# Global Productivity Mindset
## Inspire Talent & Achieve
## Exceptional Performance

*Take Vision & Mission statements*
*off the boardroom wall.*
*Put them into practice!*

First Publication 2012
Second Publication 2023

Authors:
Siddharaj V S Param & Prashant Tipnis
Winnipeg, Manitoba, CANADA

First Edition: 2012
Canada ISBN: 978-0-9879940-0-4
Printed in Canada 2012

Second Edition – Revised & Updated: 2023
Canada ISBN: 978-0-9879940-3-5
Published on amazon.com 2023

Dedicated to our families for
their continual inspiration and
support.

They show us how it is possible
to be resilient and to remain positive.

# CONTENTS

# PREFACE

*All business is global!*
*All local markets are part of the global market!*

This book provides a framework for an analysis with a fresh perspective of events leading up to 2023. This helps us understand the productivity mindset that has led us to the present environment of global trade with large numbers of middleclass in the Americas, Europe, Asia and Africa.

Friend-shoring, near-shoring and re-shoring of supply chains are buzz words that are being used to address supply chain resiliency post pandemic response. This requires a cross-cultural understanding of business practices with a global productivity mindset.

The analysis of businesses that survived the global pandemic and succeeded post pandemic reaffirmed the value of having a global productivity mindset. This inspired a revision of the book to include the relevance of resiliency and its relation to the global productivity mindset.

Over the centuries, whenever a global productivity mindset was applied to business, the result has been generation of wealth and prosperity. This same mindset can be found in grandma's kitchen and her preparation of healthy meals.

The top leadership of major corporations realize that, with the latest wave of globalization since 1989, the creation of middleclass consumers around the world represents a marketing opportunity for businesses practicing the right mindset of productivity throughout the organization.

The current wave of globalization started with the rapid development of export driven trade and local infrastructure growth initially in the tiger economies of Hong Kong, Taiwan, South Korea and South East Asia. Subsequently, the former socialist economies of Russia, China, India, Brazil and Vietnam adopted similar strategies opening up their economies to global trade and infrastructure development.

**The knowledge of these top corporate leaders can be understood by applying a qualitative analysis of business practices within individual companies. This analysis should be in the context of the social, cultural and economic realities in specific countries. The methodology for such an analysis requires a global productivity mindset.**

A global productivity mindset helps us to better understand the quantitative information documented through management systems. This mindset needs to be understood by all levels of employees including leaders, managers, administrators, supervisors and the rank and file employees.

Applying a global productivity mindset at all levels of the business organization and across departments is a necessary prerequisite for business success.

# INTRODUCTION

## Grandma's Kitchen and Her Spice Rack

Here's a story that illustrates a lesson on productivity applicable to all businesses ranging in size from a local diner to a global multinational corporate fast-food chain. It is also applicable to all types of businesses in both product and service sectors.

Ever wondered how Grandma cooked all those meals at home and still always managed a pleasant smile?

Whether she was cooking for five or fifty, her estimates would never go wrong.

She had more than her personal skills. She organized her kitchen with a mindset to make every mealtime a happy, healthy occasion. Grandma did not take courses in quality systems such as ISO or Lean or Six Sigma – she practised them.

Everything she needed was arranged in such a way that she could reach any item with the stretch of a hand. Some foods needed a mix of spices and condiments. Grandma had them all at her fingertips with her organized 'spice rack.'

A selection of ready sprinkle containers of spices, herbs and salts similar to the one grandma had is a great idea for organizing the modern kitchen for quick meal preparations with no compromise on quality, nutrition and flavor.

It appears that Grandma utilized the essence of lean principles, ethical conduct and a secret ingredient, to productively deliver quality. Some would call this secret ingredient, 'love'; others would call it 'passion' or even, 'attitude'.

We prefer to call it, 'the right mindset driven by passion'. This mindset, when applied in today's business world, can be termed as the global productivity mindset.

**_Global productivity mindset_ is comprised of the following 10 mindset ingredients which, when combined, can unleash exceptional performance from existing talents in organizations:**

Skills Resource Mindset
*Use existing resources to seize new opportunities.*

Global Picture Mindset
*Remove compartments to focus on vision, mission and goals.*

Constant Change Mindset
*Benefit from change and innovation.*

Global Economy Mindset
*Local markets are a part of the global market.*

Ethical Quality Mindset
*Create trust in products and services.*

Process Efficiency Mindset
*Benefit from a global network of finance, production and marketing.*

Productivity Motivation Mindset
*Allow the best individuals in the team to shine.*

Business Passion Mindset
*Passion is a critical component in the production cycle.*

Continual Improvement Mindset
*Create a continual profit spiral upwards.*

Global Middleclass Mindset
*Tap into global demand for quality.*

This book is organized into ten chapters, each covering an ingredient of global productivity mindset to facilitate internalizing change. By utilizing all ten ingredients, you can unleash the energy and full potential of your workforce.

## The Global Economy

The 21$^{st}$ century has seen the emergence of middleclass markets worldwide. While there is a convergence of lifestyles of this middleclass, there are also local flavours in the preferences of consumers in individual countries.

A global productivity mindset promotes universal standards which are responsive to local cultural practices and expressions. This mindset is universal on "what" must be done to achieve goals while allowing for local input with a degree of flexibility on "how" these goals are to be achieved.

Political governments built on the base of middleclass populations now act as the bankers of last resort for both the global financial and commercial markets. This middleclass provides both the productivity that drives business success and additionally constitutes the consumer base that is the source for commercial profits.

Commercial trade will continue to grow with a worldwide middleclass driving this growth. Corporations that have embraced a global productivity mindset appear to be benefiting even more from this worldwide middleclass.

*(Refer to Appendix A for further reading on the evolution of global trade over the last five centuries.)*

# GRANDMA'S KITCHEN INSPIRES
# A MODERN MANUFACTURER

There is a classic case study that students of business administration in United Kingdom enjoy discussing. The case study is about establishing of an Asian frozen food manufacturing success.

The story begins with a young migrant housewife who in the 1970s arrived in United Kingdom only to find the quality and taste of Indian foods on the local supermarket shelves appalling.

Believing that she could cook tastier foods, she began with a home kitchen operation supplying samosas to local delis and takeaways around the English town where she lived. These sold well.

Her mindset was founded on producing quality meals and her ambition was huge. She had a vision from the very beginning to have her products on the shelves of shops nationwide.

Since childhood she understood the importance of food, fresh ingredients and fantastic flavors. She attributed this understanding to her grandmother and mother.

With persistence she persuaded a major supermarket chain to accept her food products. Her only problem was she did not have a commercial manufacturing facility.

She was operating with just five women helping with the production. She was forthright with the supermarket chain about this. The supermarket waited while she raised enough capital to set up a small production facility. The business grew rapidly and after a year she needed more space.

With capital from investors, sales quickly exceeded £5 million. Business grew rapidly amid ups and downs in obtaining additional investments. In time, her frozen food company is reputed to have grown to a turnover of about £100 million a year with well over a thousand employees supplying products to supermarkets in United Kingdom and Europe.

From the kitchen to global trade to the positive experience of consumers worldwide a productivity mindset as old as the spice trade has always delivered to the satisfaction and profit of all in the supply chain.

The challenge is to internalize the productivity mindset within your organization, to profit from the business opportunities that have emerged in the past few decades.

**Embrace the Global Productivity Mindset
and thrive in the 21<sup>st</sup> century.**

## SKILLS RESOURCE MINDSET

*We need to take a fresh look at our existing resources in the context of new developments and emerging trends post global financial meltdown and post-pandemic response.*

# CHAPTER 1 – Skills Resource Mindset

Multinational corporations understand that even with a slowing domestic economy there is a growing middleclass worldwide willing to buy their products and services.

**Businesses should use existing resources to seize new opportunities.**

However, consumer focus has shifted to purchasing alternative brands, which are cheaper and are perceived to be of the same quality as the established brands.

Quality and value for money appears to be a major factor in the purchasing consciousness of the middleclass around the world. National brands are giving way to product quality, irrespective of origin.

Established brands are being challenged by new players for the consumers' choice. Quality and value for their money shapes the mindset of many middleclass consumers.

Country of manufacture is not much of a criterion in making the buying decision.

Brands need to consistently invoke quality assurance in order to remain competitive and maintain market share. This requires a mindset amongst employees throughout the organization to maintain a consistent global quality at a productive level.

The North American and European economies are working hard at maintaining stability at a stubbornly slow growth rate. Multinational corporate players based in these economies have been able to maintain or even grow profits by tapping into the consumer demand of the middleclass across the world.

Global trade has always been driven by innovation. The post World War II boom of the United States from the 1950s onwards was driven by innovation in electrical technology. This period saw the introduction of items such as the vacuum cleaner, washing machine, dish washer, radio, record player and television.

Japan joined the North America and Europe with innovations such as the transistor radio, cassette players, colored television and high fidelity music record players.

Product innovation succeeded where companies were willing to adopt new methods of production along with productivity training for employees.

Unskilled laborers armed with skills and motivational training were transformed into skilled workers who themselves became middleclass consumers.

This local market of workers in countries around the world stimulated the growth of local entrepreneurs manufacturing for local markets.

With the advent of information technology and cyber connectivity, the world is now a market for all manufacturers no matter the size of the business operations.

At the local level, professional education and leadership skills training is transforming the local middleclass through increased wealth into a global middleclass demanding global quality standards in products and services.

This transformation is growing rapidly in Asia, Africa and South America.

The role of businesses is to generate wealth through profit driven free enterprise. This has to be achieved through an organizational synergy that stimulates a global productivity mindset.

We now know that stabilizing the financial markets stabilizes the commercial markets in products and services. This allows businesses to focus on consolidating their internal organizational strengths while identifying their market niche.

It is now a global economy and an increasingly borderless world for trade. We therefore have to expect that there will be more and more suppliers of goods and providers of services who will trade worldwide.

Since it is quality and value for money that is shaping markets rather than loyalty to traditional brands, understanding what the consumer truly wants is critical to strategic business planning.

The business that understands more of the variables that shape the global consumer demand and is able to respond with a global productivity mindset will be the one to pull ahead of the competition. **It is always the team with the better strategy that wins.**

The time has come for the commercial sector around the world to look for new businesses to launch the next spurt of global economic growth. The challenge for entrepreneurs is to identify the right productivity mindset to maximize profit.

The growth of the Asia Pacific economies suggests tremendous business opportunities for those willing to explore overseas markets.

Giant US fast food chains, recognize that the rapid growth of middleclass across Asia and Africa, will mean a larger market for them than in North America.

India, China and South East Asia (which include Malaysia, Singapore, Thailand, Vietnam, Indonesia and the Philippines) as well as Africa look attractive as destinations for North American lifestyle products. There is a large middleclass consumer base that offers a huge market opportunity.

However, to succeed it is important to research the market trends and demands in these markets outside North America and Europe.

The world economy has gone global with the G20 replacing the G7 as the global economic policy organization influencing the agenda for action of the International Monetary Fund (IMF), the World Bank, the United Nations Organization (UN) and the World Trade Organization (WTO) on global financial stability and socioeconomic development.

Multinational corporations (MNCs) utilizing global purchasing and marketing strategies have reshaped all industries. This has transformed products and services into commodities traded at a global standard price. This global commodification especially of food production has created a harmonization of prices of raw materials.

A consequent saving on cost of production achieved through technological automation and skills training have further leveled the playing field as to the geographical location for manufacturing.

It is interesting to note that significant cost savings for production in China have been achieved through automation in manufacturing with Indian technology companies providing substantial software and consulting support.

The costs of transportation for goods and services have now been significantly reduced to the extent that their impact on pricing is no longer a major factor.

As a consequence of these developments, most markets for products and services have been transformed into global markets.

The economics of commercial enterprise is being driven by the quality of living aspirations of the global middleclass.

The global middleclass expect to live in urban environments that provide world class quality standards in education, healthcare, income, pension, consumer goods, leisure lifestyle and happiness.

There is concern about environmental disaster preparedness and response in the event of natural calamities such as earthquakes, floods, tornadoes and climate change. This is stimulating expectations in product and service innovation and design that the middleclass desire to see the economy and industry provide.

Food security in the context of affordable, nutritious and tasty meals in settings with pleasant ambience is another area where the middleclass expectations are growing.

Alternative energy technology supplementing traditional fossil fuel sources is another area of economic activity ripe with commercial opportunity.

Economic models that are sustainable and renewable create a feel good factor for consumers by making them believe they are doing the right thing while enjoying the product or service.

Fair trade models and corporate responsibility initiatives create trust and confidence in brands and corporations which in turn influences consumer choice. They also encourage pride in employees who then become more productive with the mindset, that doing the right thing for the company means doing it better for the community.

The net result is that, the employee productivity goes up, quality of products is enhanced and the consumer is willing to pay a premium in price.

When it comes to products and services, the middleclass is indifferent as to whether these are provided through private or public initiative. The determining factor is efficient delivery at a competitive price.

For employees to acquire a global productivity mindset they need education and skills training while being kept informed of the company's performance.

This requires a management information system that keeps employees updated on the performance of the business as a whole.

Socioeconomic success comes from having a sound regulatory framework that promotes equity and opportunities for individuals, to achieve a high quality of living founded on health, education and happiness for all.

Business success comes from the ability of individuals to internalize a productivity mindset, which drives the organization to profit financially, while increasing the self-esteem of the individual.

Trends in sustainability can emerge through research and development. For instance, in Malaysia, wood obtained from rubber plantations is being used for manufacture of furniture, thus saving the forest. This has created pride in employees within the furniture manufacturing industry in Malaysia.

**Actionable Takeaway:**

**To build positive brand perception, invest in developing a "skills resource mindset".**

# GLOBAL PICTURE MINDSET

*We need to go beyond the attitude of departments operating within boxes, busily ticking off boxes in a check list, thereby missing the big picture of the vision, mission and goals of the organization.*

## CHAPTER 2 – Global Picture Mindset

Productivity requires a holistic approach to policy implementation and systems architecture design. It requires an understanding of business culture and ethical conduct.

**Businesses should remove internal compartments to focus on achieving the vision, mission and goals.**

The rising middleclass represents the increasing intellectual capital for business innovation and a growing consumer market for products and services produced in a sustainable manner.

Here is a story of how informal talks in common areas led to a holistic approach in the allocation of annual expense budgets in a large company.

At the budget meeting, while most departmental leaders were busy defending their respective estimates, one particular leader was able to suggest savings in other departments that could lead to reallocating of funds to his department.

Investigations on how he was able to gather the information that gave the big picture, led to a simple fact, that he was able to utilize the informal information to get the big picture understanding of the budget.

The practice of many successful companies has been to encourage managers and staff to utilize the common cafeteria for meals. This fosters camaraderie amongst employees and encourages sharing of information. The shared information often leads to a holistic approach in problem solving.

**Vision and mission statements must come off the boardroom walls and be instilled into the workforce as a global productivity mindset driving the organization.**

In this context, grandma's vision of serving healthy foods would lead to cooks being retrained as chefs. They would thus become more productive, serving quality. Consumers may live longer and return to eat smaller servings paying a premium for delicious healthy meals.

Extending the same mindset to the textile industry would lead to questions such as, 'Do we earn more by selling one $500/- designer Tee shirt or selling one hundred $5/- Tee shirts made with unskilled labor?'

About half the world's population is considered to be middleclass. The emergence of this worldwide middleclass has essentially been due to rapid economic growth outside of the G7 economies. This growth has primarily been in the emerging and newly emerged economies of Asia, Eastern Europe, South America and Africa.

The middleclass is defined as those individuals, who have a residual discretionary income after paying for the necessities of life such as food, shelter and clothing. They live above the subsistence level of the poor. They have the money to buy improved healthcare, education and consumer goods for their families.

A large percentage of the middleclass population in the emerging and newly emerged economies is middleclass by the standards of those economies. This local middleclass has income below those living in the established economies of the G7 countries.

There is also a global middleclass in the emerging and emerged economies whose income is equivalent to those in the established economies. However it is pertinent to note that the local middleclass in Asia, Eastern Europe, South America and Africa collectively outnumber the middleclass in the G7 economies.

At the same time that we see a rapid expansion of the middleclass in Asia, there appears to be a shrinking of the middleclass base in North America brought on by consumer debts and the insufficient retraining of the workforce.

The captive markets in the Asian countries may be bigger than the export market for many Asian businesses.

The emergence of a middleclass around the world has been very rapid since the 1980s. This has redefined the global economy into three regions.

We now have a region, which can be characterized as established, with the majority of the population being global middleclass.

There is another region, which can be characterized as the emerged region where there is a significant number of the population who are either global or local middleclass.

A third region of the world can be characterized as emerging, where the majority of the population aspires to be middleclass.

These three regions are not geographical in nature, but are rather identified by the numbers of the middleclass population residing therein.

The 2008 financial crisis has put financial pressures, more on the middleclass, than on the poor and the rich in the European and North American economies. The consumer credit market may have created a false economy.

Workers are the middleclass consumers who drive the commercial economy. So we should treat workers like we treat customers.

The turnaround of the North American automobile industry came from a refocusing on productivity serving the customers. The lesson we learn is, ultimately business is about getting paying customers.

As technology and infrastructure cost pushes up the cost of living, business competitiveness can only be achieved through skills training that creates a higher productivity level that maintains the worker as a consumer.

Take the case of a labor-intensive European factory that uses 100 unskilled workers. Introducing automation that requires only 2 skilled workers to run a computerized robotic factory can be seen as progress that leads to 98 individuals losing work.

The other side of the coin requires us to provide skills training that will allow the 100 workers to run 50 automated factories while earning higher salaries to afford the additional goods reaching the market at a lower cost.

A global productivity mindset requires that we see skilled workers as both more productive staff as well as potential consumers of our products. In the long run technology creates greater opportunities and is not a threat to businesses.

Sound financial systems can provide investment capital for businesses that innovate and create products utilizing new technology.

The 1990s saw a rapid growth trajectory take hold in South East Asia. A particular mattress manufacturing company, with an eye for the global export market, decided to pledge all its property for bank financing in order to automate their factory. Computers were used to run the manufacturing for production of world class mattresses. Unfortunately, the Asian financial crisis hit and the company was unable to service its bank loans due to reduced cash flow from poor sales volumes. This made it insolvent.

Here was a company that was run by the third generation owners who were highly knowledgeable in operational management and marketing. However, they did not understand the financial risk the company was being exposed to by putting all their eggs into one national economic basket.

They had a clear vision of becoming a global manufacturing company with the mission to export globally. Unfortunately, the board of directors did not understand the high risk involved in utilizing domestic loan financing.

An analysis of the local political, economic, social and technological factors (PEST analysis) could have helped the company directors realize the high risk of not utilizing the global advantage of leveraging financing from an established economy in order to manufacture in South East Asia for the global export market.

A global productivity mindset compels us to adopt a holistic approach in financial, operational and marketing planning.

An interesting illustration of utilizing a global productivity mindset in manufacturing is the experience of a corporation in multicultural Canada.

The directors who were shareholders had a sound knowledge of the Asian market for the company's products. By leveraging the research and development opportunities available in Canada the corporation was able to raise financing from the financial markets in Toronto to manufacture in Asia for the Asian market.

This arrangement illustrates how a Canadian corporation can prosper by utilizing its intellectual capital to raise financial capital at a lower financial risk in Canada for its operations in Asia for sales in the growing Asian market.

**Actionable Takeaway:**

**To benefit from business opportunities, implement a "global picture mindset" and remove compartmentalization across job functions.**

# CONSTANT CHANGE MINDSET

*We need to understand that the only thing permanent is change and that innovation and new technologies are emerging across geographical boundaries.*

## CHAPTER 3 – Constant Change Mindset

Global trade has leveled the playing field for business, and innovation can emerge from anywhere in the world.

**A mind open to change and innovation is best placed to benefit from market opportunities.**

Since the invention of the wheel in the Stone Age, man has relied on innovation for progress. Just imagine the world without the inventions and discoveries in the fields of material and biological sciences. There would be no ships but for the understanding of the laws of buoyancy; no airplanes without the knowledge of laws of gravity; no modern antibiotics without the discovery of penicillin and no nuclear energy as an alternate fuel without the atomic theory.

Today's world is depending heavily on technology and innovation. Man reached the moon about fifty years ago, having launched into space in the early 1950s. Since the advent of computers, technology has developed by leaps and bounds.

A 10 year old child in today's world may not be aware of what a typewriter looks like. The case mentioned in the previous chapter referred to a chemical blending factory in Europe which was fully automated in the 1980s. The raw material feed was automated and so was the finished product canning and palletizing. The quality sampling was randomly selected by the computer program. The factory only needed a couple of highly skilled workers to control the operations.

The manufacturing world has advanced much further in the use of technology. The super computers and the computer assisted robots can achieve complex tasks at a pace much higher than humans. However, are they capable of research and development? Are they innovators? The human element with the right mindset is still vital, even with the advent of artificial intelligence.

Research and development requires transparency. It is important to note two types of transparency:

- The first being transparency based on contract amongst business partners.

- The second type of transparency critical for research and development is the transparency within 'Centers of Excellence' where there is free exchange of information amongst industry peers.

Innovation is defined as the application of technology in a novel way. In the 19th century Thomas Edison's electrical inventions were patented. These intellectual capital creations were successfully utilized through business enterprise to generate vast profits.

To commercialize the intellectual capital created through innovation, it is important to locate centers of excellence in jurisdictions that protect patents, designs, trademarks and copyrights.

A secret ingredient for many a business success has been an investment in product development and constant experimenting. It is everyone's responsibility to come up with new ideas – it can be in design, packaging or processing.

Every business should keep innovating and raising the bar with new product lines.

The global outlook has added a geographical dimension to the supply chain. Innovation and technology are no longer domains of the traditional established economies.

President Obama while in office, stressed that for the US it is a "Sputnik moment" that challenges American industry to go to the next level of technology.

**Actionable Takeaway:**

**Stimulate innovation and positive change by adopting a "constant change mindset" that transforms the business into a center of excellence.**

# GLOBAL ECONOMY MINDSET

*We need to understand that all business is global and that the labels such as emerging, emerged or established economies may not give natural advantages in the creation of global brands.*

# CHAPTER 4 – Global Economy Mindset

After the Second World War, from 1945 onwards into the 1960s, the North Atlantic economies of North America and Western Europe began to grow rapidly with government funding of health, education, housing and free trade in goods and services.

This led to demand for raw commodities from Asia and Africa. Research and development led to innovations that stimulated the growth of business in creating and supplying consumer goods and services to the growing North American and Western European middleclass.

**In essence, all local markets have become a part of one global market.**

Japan started to rebuild its' economy by encouraging corporations to go into the business of infrastructure development and manufacturing.

Incentives for research and development saw Japanese corporations initially manufacture for Japan's middleclass. Subsequently they started exporting to the North American, European and emerging Asian markets.

From the 1960s onwards North American, European and Japanese companies began to set up factories in what came to be known as the Asian Tiger economies of Hong Kong, Taiwan and South East Asia.
From this point on the label "made in (a specified country)" became irrelevant as quality came to be associated with a brand name in the eyes of the consumer.

This allowed Japanese corporations to effectively compete with MNCs from the European Economic Community (EEC) and North America. The seven largest of these economies came to be known as the G7 countries.

From the 1980s onwards corporations from the Asian Tiger economies of Taiwan and South Korea, through innovation, began competing effectively with corporations from the G7.

Japan, Taiwan and South Korea have shown that the key to creating a global brand acceptable to middleclass consumers is innovation and productivity in manufacturing quality products.

A culture of innovation changes the behavior of employees through the inculcating of a global productivity mindset resulting in the creation of globally recognized brands.

Trade liberalization within the EEC and North America especially between the US and Canada created a middleclass skilled workforce able to deliver at high productivity levels that offset the increased wages due to increased cost of living in Europe and North America.

Initially, labor intensive production was shifted to Asian Tiger economies. The subsidiaries of G7 based MNCs operating in Asian and South American countries provided skills training for their local employees. This transformed unskilled labor in Asia and South America into a pool of skilled local middleclass.

These were people who were middleclass by the standards of their local national economy having disposable income to spend on education, health and consumer goods manufactured locally. This stimulated the establishment of local businesses manufacturing for local national consumer markets.

With free trade being promoted from the 1980s onwards and the establishing of the World Trade Organization (WTO), trade began expanding with countries like China, India and Russia. The lowering of tariffs between nations encouraged internal private sector development.

The successes of the Asian Tiger economies are now being replicated in most countries in the world. This is moving large numbers of people worldwide into the local middleclass of local economies.

From the 1980s onwards, increasing numbers of professionals and entrepreneurs in Asia, South America, Russia and Africa began moving towards providing global quality products and services with the adopting of a global productivity mindset.

These professionals and entrepreneurs earn global levels of income commensurate to that earned by their counterparts in North America, Japan and Europe thereby bringing them within the fold of a global middleclass able to afford the best quality products offered by the most innovative corporations.

This global middleclass is now found in significant numbers in almost every country in the world but in greater numbers in the top 20 economies of the world.

The 1997 Asian financial crisis is believed to have been caused by bursting of the bubble created from very rapid growth in the Asian Tiger economies. The finance ministers and central bankers of the G20 largest established and emerged economies in the world came together and stabilized the economies of the affected countries.

The G20 came together again in 2010 in Toronto, Canada to strengthen the stabilization measures undertaken after the 2008 global financial crisis. The 2008 crisis is said to have started with the collapse in confidence resulting from the uncertain nature of derivative trading by bankers in New York.

The global middleclass around the world remain a very lucrative market for businesses selling global quality products and services. To tap into this wealthy market requires a willingness to venture beyond traditional markets across oceans.

For North American businesses the Asian markets west of the West Coast are once again an inviting business destination.

It is time to complete the journey started by Christopher Columbus.

Free trade allows both big and small businesses, offering quality products and services, to cash in on the demands for quality by the global middleclass worldwide. This is because the cost of global trade is going down with supply chains able to reach all parts of the globe.

To continue serving the middleclass, manufacturers are rebalancing supply chain efficiency with supply chain resilience.

Additionally, manufacturers should look for sales opportunities among the rapidly growing middleclass in Asia. Middle east, Africa and South America.

Local manufacturers in G20 countries will have to adopt a global productivity mindset of continual improvement to compete with the falling prices of imported products.

The prices of food and other cost of living items are going up worldwide. This is forcing a demand for higher wages that can only be justified through productivity improvement. This can lead to an upward spiral of better quality products which higher wage earners will be able to afford.

This dynamics is encouraging the growth in numbers of global middleclass consumers from the ranks of the local middleclass.

For local businesses to survive, they must acquire a global productivity mindset to retain their share of the local or regional market even if they do not wish to export.

The practice of local businesses producing local quality for the local market protected by national tariffs against foreign competitors is being dismantled quite rapidly.

For MNCs entering a local market, setting up a subsidiary along with establishing its own distributorship network requires the training of local staff to ensure a global productivity mindset.

Appointing a local distributor may be a cheaper option initially. However, this may not result in the distributor acquiring the necessary global productivity mindset on its own. It is essential that the manufacturer ensures that the local distributor's staff are trained to a level reflecting a global productivity mindset.

The reality of free trade is that local businesses will have to compete with global players for local, regional and global markets.

Global trade has long shifted manufacturing from established to the emerged economies. However, innovation now allows businesses in emerged economies to project a global image that competes effectively with established brands from established economies.

As the ranks of the global middleclass grow worldwide, geographical location may no longer be a significant cost factor for businesses adopting a global productivity mindset.

Instead the political, economic, social and technological (PEST) certainties will increasingly be significant factors on where to locate the financial, innovation and production centers.

The success of the Asian Tiger economies from the 1960s onwards was primarily due to their ability to provide stable political and economic infrastructure for MNCs to manufacture for export back to their home countries.

**The PEST analysis remains encouraging for North American innovation and financing of production in Asia for the global market.** The cases mentioned in chapter three illustrate the advantage of leveraging the global realities.

The British East India Company is generally considered as the first modern MNC with offices, branches and manufacturing facilities in different countries controlled by headquarters in London, England.

The East India Company and other companies based in London, England traded across Asia from India to Ceylon, Malaya and Singapore. It built infrastructure such as roads, railways and ports; provided staff quarters, provision stores and schools; and even funded cultural festivals.

These activities, in support of trading activities for profit, touched the lives of the employees and their communities so much that many local people referred to government in general as, "the Company". Here we see the Company creating a local middleclass consumer market for goods from England through its own activities.

Cheap labor is on its way out as a productivity advantage as workers worldwide seek skills that will earn them the salary that provides a middleclass consumer lifestyle. Additionally, the demand for quality products are best met through automation of processes operated by skilled personnel.

The shift towards a global productivity mindset worldwide will see increased market opportunities for businesses big and small. This shift will also see the increasing growth of a global middleclass emerging from the local middleclass around the world.

Such a development can only translate into greater profits for businesses as the wealth of nations grow with increased global trade.

**Actionable Takeaway:**

**Utilize a "Global Economy Mindset" to balance supply chain efficiency with supply chain resilience. This will help you to remain competitive in your existing market with a prospect to expand into wider markets.**

## ETHICAL QUALITY MINDSET

*We need to understand that consumers worldwide are demanding quality, which can only be sustained over the long term through ethical leadership that translates into trust in the products and services.*

## CHAPTER 5 – Ethical Quality Mindset

We have seen that, adhering to work ethics, fair competition and productivity principles have led to tremendous growth for MNCs. Unfortunately, an overemphasis on financial profits as a driving force in business has too often resulted in rapid growth and sudden collapses.

**Ethical business conduct builds trust in products and services.**

History teaches us that honesty is still the best policy when it comes to sustaining long term growth. The case illustrations in this book show that it is critical to be honest and principled for survival and success during major economic upheavals. Business leaders who exhibit these traits are the ones who are respected and most admired.

Leaders who are initially perceived as awkward, untalented, unworthy of the job and out of depth can prove their critics wrong by adopting a global productivity mindset.

During the 1990s, new businesses emerged from nowhere, when the MNCs started to outsource their information technology needs. These MNCs tapped into overseas talent with a global mindset. This sparked a boom in the information technology sector and subsequently spread to the other businesses in India.

An important business maxim is, "a promise is a promise". Holding to this maxim, established business conglomerates have been able to diversify into non-traditional areas of business and succeed. Reinventing yourself is always an option in business.

The standards of quality demanded by the global middleclass require an understanding that quality assurances are intimately linked to brand perception.

**The old company maxim of, "maximum financial profits for the shareholders" has, now been modified to "maximum human and financial profits for the stakeholders".** This is because most of the stakeholders come from the ranks of the consuming middleclass.

Labor standards established in the MNC's home country should also be applied in overseas operations to avoid negative perceptions by consumers.

The collapsing of Rana Plaza in Bangladesh resulted in huge death toll in a factory manufacturing garments for prominent global brands. The incidence tarnished the image of these brands with consumers in North America and Europe.

With global middleclass markets growing across the Asian and African continents the need to comply with acceptable standards becomes increasingly important.

The handling of the Bhopal chemical leak tragedy which saw such horrific loss of lives in this Indian town is believed to have tainted the image of MNCs from the established economies in general amongst the wider Indian population. This perception has lingered and may be contributing even now to the vocal opposition to entry into the Indian market, especially of MNCs from established economies.

**Perception is very important and the brand value, which represents the quality and pricing of the product, needs to be safeguarded by a strong emphasis on ethics in the work place.**

The Bhopal tragedy has ingrained the importance of ethical business conduct into the minds of workers, consumers and communities around the world.

Business ethics now must deal with issues of health and safety, sustainable development and action to prevent negative environmental impact.

When ethical issues are addressed openly with stakeholders, it feeds into the global productivity mindset that leads to greater productivity by the workforce. The employees will take pride in claiming ownership of processes. This process ownership encourages feedback that leads to continual improvement and innovation.

It is important to note that the emerged economies have been implementing integrated development plans. This has created townships complete with modern homes shopping malls, schools, hospitals and entertainment centers with water, electricity, sanitation, roads, and public transit systems.

These developments have raised the expectations of the local population. Many are now aspiring for skilled jobs and middleclass quality of living.

In today's global economy, innovation is driving business growth. The right business environment needs to be created for long term success.

We find the innovators of information technology companies moving to locations such as Silicon Valley in California, USA primarily to remain stimulated by the spirit of innovation that a concentration of talents creates.

Vancouver, Canada is another such location that attracts a concentration of talent that has earned it the nickname, "Hollywood North". Its West Coast lifestyle encourages natural and organic growers to experiment and come up with healthy eating options for the growing health conscious consumer market worldwide.

The emerged middleclass of emerging economies such as those in Brazil, Russia, India, China and South Africa (BRICS) are now contributing to the demand for quality and innovation helping North American MNCs to continue to grow and profit.

The advantage that these MNCs bring to the BRICS economies is similar to what they contributed to the Asian Tiger economies in the 1980s.

They have introduced an efficient supply chain delivery system that gives the middleclass in the BRICS economies global quality experiences. This is made possible by the utilization of a global productivity mindset that takes into account the rising wages in these economies.

Any business, no matter the size, can take advantage of these global opportunities by integrating a global productivity mindset into its business culture. The modern supply chain and information technology supports businesses of all sizes.

A particular case in point is of a bakery specializing in rich fruit cakes operating in a town in the US. Utilizing the power of internet, it is able to promote quality festive cakes worldwide. The cakes are delivered through the use of courier services. Over the years the bakery created loyal customers that trust the quality of their cakes. **This bakery is able to operate as a micro multinational business by adopting a global productivity mindset.**

The reality today is that, the metropolitan cities such as Dubai, Mumbai and Shanghai have effectively become emerged markets.

Global wealth flows from all over the world into financial markets such as New York where they finance research and development in centers of excellence in North America. This has led to innovations for products to be manufactured in Asia for global markets.

This is made possible through the adoption of management systems to run global operations based on a global productivity mindset. Cheap labor is on its way out in the emerged markets. Creating skilled specialists is an important factor in maintaining a sustainable system for profit generation.

Trust in such a system of wealth generation with financing, innovation, manufacturing and distribution across the world is only possible with the adoption of a mindset reflecting productivity values.

These values come from the lifestyle expectations of the global middleclass, which is converging across the world. **Differences are more in the form of local flavors and cultural expression of a universal expectation.** Hence, convergence of lifestyles shapes consumer demand and impacts on the productivity mindset.

The internet has created a web of consumer and employee interactions that are increasingly reshaping workplace expectations and attitudes.

No longer is communication across the world being conducted only by a limited number of top level executives of MNCs. The cost of internet and mobile phone communication now allows all staff to communicate with counterparts across the world.

It therefore becomes an advantage for businesses to tap into the feedback available from their staff from all levels of the business organization.

Good news as well as bad news can now spread "virally' worldwide within minutes. It is therefore vital to channel this reality in a manner that benefits the business by shaping a course of action that takes care of the needs of all stakeholders.

**Actionable Takeaway:**

**Adopting a "Global Ethical Mindset" leads to employee enthusiasm in delivering quality products that build customer confidence and loyalty.**

# PROCESS EFFICIENCY MINDSET

*We need to understand that in order to deliver efficient business processes, the geographical location of research & development, financing, production, marketing and sales may be dispersed worldwide with information technology establishing a seamless connection within a global organizational network.*

## CHAPTER 6 – Process Efficiency Mindset

MNCs tend to utilize global vision and mission within the context of local production and distribution networks. The global vision and mission is implemented at the shop floor through a process that allows for local ownership.

This facilitates global ethics and systems integrity to tap into local skills and talent, resulting in local solutions to local problems.

**There is tremendous benefit from utilizing a global network of finance, production and marketing.**

Look inside the components of a car, television or computer and you will find parts made in several countries by several different businesses whom we often consider to be competitors in sales of the finished products.

Global supply chains have ensured the availability of components to different parts of world. Various companies have set up their research and development centers in countries far from the manufacturing sites. This is all possible because of ease of transfer of technology as well as improved transportation systems.

A recent development in this context is cloud computing.

The diversity of markets arising from customer demographics is considered a positive challenge to sales and marketing.

MNCs utilize the model of global vision where manufacturing sites are established to cater for local customer needs. The technology may be centralized as may be the worldwide distribution.

Companies that aim to become world class organizations need to develop internal champions who can support and lead various initiatives and continuous improvement teams.

Implementation of continuous improvement initiatives requires a global productivity mindset that recognizes the importance of understanding cultural differences and local talent.

Quality systems help in standardizing the processes so that products manufactured in different parts of the world may be used locally. As a result standardization in materials and processes has encouraged the migration of quality skilled workforce from emerging to the established economies.

**A global productivity mindset requires qualitative thinking based on passion and objectivity in interpreting quantitative data.**

Competitiveness requires a system that utilizes skills to integrate global business cultures and middleclass consumer expectations. This stimulates behaviour that results in productivity.

It is a challenge to standardize quality, due to variables in the business environment such as location, culture and infrastructure. Global outlook demands a uniform way of thinking before acting.

Here is a case that illustrates the relationship between central, regional and local organization for research and development (R & D) as well as procurement of ingredients for manufacturing.

A European MNC functioned with a three tier organization of their research and development and procurement departments. The core research and development was carried out at the central laboratories for products that could be distributed worldwide. The purchasing for such products was carried out by the central purchasing department.

At the regional level, research and development catered for products uniquely required within the region. For these products, procurement was done at the regional level.

In addition, some local research and development was carried out to accommodate to the peculiar country needs. Local sourcing fulfilled the local requirements.

The interesting point about this arrangement was that the global vision and mission of the MNC ensured a two way communication of information within the three tiers. This ensured an operational synergy based on a global productivity mindset.

**Once the processes are standardized across the globe, it does not matter where the components are manufactured. Final assembly is just a matter of connecting the dots to solve the puzzle.**

Quality systems have evolved over the years to accommodate for the changing business environment. ISO systems provided a step towards standardization of processes. Lean manufacturing induced productivity improvements from within.

Emphasis was given to culture change, attitude and training to develop employees into productivity champions. Employees were empowered by making them process owners. Productivity parameters were set using 'world class' requirements.

Most of the organizations that survived and progressed post 2008 global financial meltdown and the subsequent global pandemic lock-down had implemented ingredients of the global productivity mindset.

**Actionable Takeaway:**

**Utilize 'Process Efficiency Mindset' to develop internal champions and allow for process ownership to continually deliver quality products and services.**

## PRODUCTIVITY MOTIVATION MINDSET

*We need to understand the productivity motivators that allow the best individuals in the team to shine.*

# CHAPTER 7 - Productivity Motivation Mindset

**Allow the best individuals in the team to shine.**

Leaders may not be the best individual performers in the team but are the best motivators for the team.

How true! We often notice this phenomenon on the sports field. The captain is not necessarily the best player in the team. As a matter of fact, it has been observed that the best player is not always as successful when made captain.

To analyze this incongruence, we must understand the difference in attributes of a player and that of a captain.

A player is often a specialist in a position with definite personal goals, while a captain is a strategist and a people person looking after team goals. This equates to the roles of employees, supervisors and managers in the business environment. When placed in the right position, individuals can utilize their talent and achieve exceptional performance.

Employees are specialists or professionals, supervisors are people persons and managers are strategists. This has been true for all ages, but globalization has changed the way businesses are managed.

There are more demographic and geographic variations to the businesses today. A manager from Asia with education in Europe may have to manage an organization or department in North America with employees from all over the world.

Multiculturalism is the new defining word. A leader in this new world needs to be aware of differences in education, cultural upbringing, ethnicities, language variations and much more.

The 1990s saw the development of energy trading derivatives in the US.

One particular corporation grew very rapidly in this sector by hiring some of the brightest graduates from leading universities with a personality type similar to that of the Chairman and the CEO who were both very intelligent, highly qualified, and with a strong drive to achieve targets.

Both, the Chairman and the CEO strongly believed in measuring success by achievement of quarterly targets. This, they believed, could be achieved through employees possessing a similar personality.

Those individuals who succeeded were rewarded handsomely, while those who failed found themselves leaving the organization.

Older staff, who could have contributed their years of wisdom in other ways, were made redundant. They were seen as dead wood.

The financial success of the corporation led to the purchase of a utility management company in Europe. However, when the derivatives market collapsed, the now insolvent corporation, found itself selling off their European investment to Asian investors.

The new investors hired the key personnel from the utility management company as consultants and revived the business. The consultants succeeded by putting together a team of employees with the necessary competence to run the various departments.

The European team managed the business while, the investors focused on the broader vision and mission. This was in stark contrast to the approach of the US corporation that overemphasized the need for single personality type and zeal for short-term targets. A global productivity mindset by the European company helped build a team with diverse skills and personalities subscribing to a common vision.

What are productivity motivators and why do we need motivation?

Gone are the days when one would be satisfied or stimulated with a small addition to his or her personal take home wages. Managers and employees started looking forward to perks such as company owned cars and also to bonuses for that extra motivation.

Employees would look up to managers for providing the necessary motivation. In effect, employee performance was management controlled.

In today's context, the above personal motivators are inadequate.

Other lifestyle enhancing incentives are taking over. Some common examples being work from home, family time, training and development, and flexi-time.

Many successful companies, especially in the information technology sector, have moved away from traditional nine-to-five regimented culture.

Some have invested into campuses with environments that stimulate creativity. Others offer 'me time', where employees are encouraged to work on their own pet projects.

The establishing of campuses induces employees to create teams, buy into the vision of the company and take ownership of the work processes. Such adaptations to work culture attract the talent who succeed in creating exciting products.

Advanced media and technology such as videoconferencing has reduced the need for in-person meetings. **The brain drain has been replaced by a global brain network.**

Productivity improvement has gone beyond the traditional man hours per unit ratio. **In today's world, productivity is linked to the value addition an individual makes to the business.**

Additionally, non-personal incentives such as health and safety awareness at workplaces, environmental participation, and ready availability of product and process information act as physical and psychophysical stimulants of productivity.

Another major contributor to productivity is transparency in business. Transparency is easy to say but difficult to implement unless you have an outsider's view giving a fresh perspective.

Vision and mission statements are no longer statements to impress customers, but should be means to enlighten all individuals in the business. This can make the global productivity mindset your business culture.

As the business culture changes, employees will start thinking of ways of further improvement and this cycle will start rolling by itself.

Global productivity mindset acknowledges that you need transparency and ownership or your skilled workers may abandon ship at the critical time during a downturn. Headhunters may lure them away with lucrative offers leaving you with less productive staff.

A case in point involves a well diversified organization having manufacturing in Africa and South East Asia. The operational and financial headquarters were situated in Europe.

It was a family owned conglomerate of businesses with a single global vision. Although, organizationally the individual businesses were separate entities, the global vision of the owners defined and shaped the mindset of employees throughout the group.

The owners were active in policy formulation at the Board of Directors level. However the management teams including the CEO of individual business units were professionals in their respective areas of responsibility.

The reports on individual activities of the conglomerate were consolidated on a periodic basis and shared amongst the management teams of the entire group. This arrangement fostered a sense of ownership and transparency throughout the group.

It is important to rebuild your organization from the ground upwards giving ownership in process to your employees. This helps create profits for the business for all to share.

The pyramids were built from the bottom up and they are still standing thousands of years later. However, their greatest weakness was using slave labor that ran away at the first opportunity.

When the going gets tough, companies should get going to up-grade skills to motivate and improve productivity in order to stay competitive.

An individual with knowledge of the latest skills is a motivated individual. Training should focus on transforming unskilled employees into motivated skilled workers through changing the mindset throughout the business.

For large businesses, brand perception tends to be a motivator for Board directors and senior managers. In entrepreneur owned and operated businesses where the focus is on customers, motivation comes from customer satisfaction.

In both cases, pride in service needs to be re-enforced by communicating the business values to managers and employees. The ethics of process ownership and transparency impact on belief systems, changing mindsets that motivate towards better performance.

Quality and productivity systems over the years have been applied primarily as tools for employee involvement in overall functioning of the business.

From our study of several organic and whole food producers, we find a number of successful entrepreneur driven organizations. With the demand growing in this sector, the challenge for many of these businesses is to evolve into brand driven success stories.

Global productivity mindset requires us to focus on transforming the business culture.

**Actionable Takeaway:**

**Utilize the 'Productivity Motivation Mindset' to identify and attract the best talent; recognize potential leaders; and, motivate the team.**

## BUSINESS PASSION MINDSET

*We need to understand that, no matter the size of the organization, all business is global as multinationals compete with local mom & pop stores making passion a critical component in the production cycle.*

## CHAPTER 8 – Business Passion Mindset

You may not be able to compete on pricing but you can compete on the quality of service and product knowledge.

This requires motivation through sparking of passion in all individuals in the business.

**Passion is a critical component in the production cycle.**

The human story of sacrifice, perseverance, and determination to succeed against all odds is always a captivating story that resonates with most individuals.

We need to infect everyone with the passion for excellence and productivity which the founding owner used to create a business success. The founder's passion can be transmitted to employees at all levels by giving them ownership of processes.

This moves employees away from a complacent mechanical attitude expressed by an often heard remark on the shop floor, "Oh! I did it this way because the boss wanted it done this way".

You may not own a luxury car but you can come to own one by becoming a sales person for luxury cars. This is because the mindset of a successful sales person has to be similar to the mindset of his customer to be able to sell the car to the customer.

Once you have the mindset of a person who can afford to own a luxury car you can earn enough to own one yourself.

Similarly in the production shop floor, if you assemble a luxury car like the designer intended to, you will become infected with the passion of the designer and the management.

Having the passion to assemble a car that can win a grand prix race ignites the passion of a winner in the employee doing the assembly.

The story is told of an individual who wanted to own a tropical island. He could not afford one, but was sure that a market existed. Through learning and skills training, he became a real estate sales person specializing in the sale of tropical islands to high net worth individuals. This earned him enough money to ultimately own and retire to a tropical island.

We have to think global even if we do not want to go global with the business. This is because competitors down the road may be utilizing a global productivity advantage that only comes with a global mindset.

All successful entrepreneurs start by giving their local market a world-class product and service.

The frozen food producer in our case illustration started by selling the best quality Indian samosas in the local stores of the English town in which she lived. By doing this she was operating with the mindset of supplying global quality to a local market. You cannot go wrong with such an attitude.

**Passion makes up for limited resources.**

What makes Grandma successful in her cooking although there are no financial gains to be sought? It is the passion that she puts in her cooking.

Every successful product is a result of passion. For succeeding in business, we need passion at all levels.

Employees need to be passionate about their jobs, managers should be passionate about the organizational well being, and customers should be passionate about the products.

It is the passion that transformed a housewife's home business into a multimillion dollar food industry.

**When a skilled worker takes ownership of the process, efficiency and quality of output increases**

**exponentially.** The employee is now putting his heart into the job. The process is no longer a duty for him but becomes a passion.

The mindset changes from 8 hours of duty to excellence in work.

We have seen corner stores near large supermarkets having thriving business, although they do not possess the range of products which the supermarket is providing. In such cases the attention the owner pays to details about individual customers wins over.

The passion to satisfy every customer gives competitive advantage. We enjoy having our coffee at a local coffee and doughnut place rather than at a nearby international café chain. This is because we like the way the owner remembers how each of us likes our coffee. We notice that he remembers the individual preferences of each of his regular customers. His passion to serve individual taste has made many a loyal customer.

This does not mean that large businesses do not have passion. The passion however is directed towards business and the primary focus is on increasing turnover and improving profits.

Small businesses, while retaining the same goal, are more concerned about individual customer needs and maintaining long term relations.

The man who mass produced the first affordable car had the vision and passion to improve the lifestyle of society as a whole.

This vision moved society from the horse drawn carriage to the use of motorcars. It also created the eight hour work day by dividing the 24 hours in a day into three production shift cycles. In one stroke, his passion improved working conditions and increased productivity in manufacturing.

The pioneer behind the cheapest car in the world was driven by the passion to provide safe wheels for a family of four in India. People would often endanger lives by riding the entire family of husband, wife and two children on a two-wheeler.

He decided not to use an existing product model. He did not cheapen a car; instead he infected his engineers with the passion to develop a car with only the necessary components. He in essence, adopted a global productivity mindset that can be termed lean engineering.

Actionable Takeaway:

Adopt a 'Business Passion Mindset' to stimulate the passion for excellence. This will enable you to deliver world-class products and services to local markets.

# CONTINUAL IMPROVEMENT MINDSET

*We need to accept that change requires a global productivity mindset based on a continual improvement profit spiral upwards.*

# CHAPTER 9 – Continual Improvement Mindset

Grandma practiced productivity because it was an integral part of her mindset. Everyday is today and we need tomorrow's solution today.

Notice how Grandma always asked, "Did you enjoy the food". This feedback allowed her to go into a continuous improvement spiral delighting you by customizing the next meal to your satisfaction.

Change is the only constant. Accepting change is necessary but not always easy.

**Aim for continual improvement spiraling upward rather than closed loop changes.**

Development and progress of mankind over the years has followed the upward spiral. What was excellent a few years back may not be acceptable in the present day.

Each new concept should lead to another concept that transforms society. Innovation is a creation of services and products that leads to transformation in society.

The invention of the light bulb started a continual improvement and innovation cycle that has led to the creation of one of the largest corporations in the world.

This continual development spiral gave us the gramophone, washing machine, electric stove, vacuum cleaner and other household products. Each product although different, transformed the homes and lifestyle.

Similarly, information technology made popular the personal computer, notebook, digital download of music, smart phones, tablet computers, web television and cloud computing. Each product naturally leading to next one and all transforming the way we access education, work and entertainment.

Japan and Korea had the vision to strategize improvements which transformed them from the ashes of war to economic powerhouses.

Today a local business can take advantage of applying a global mindset in utilizing the best locations worldwide for production, raising of financial capital and marketing.

A business can be established in North America to take advantage of the excellent infrastructure of transportation, urban living environment, education, skills training and multiculturalism. This will attract the best talents from all over the world.

This can then be leveraged in the financial markets in New York for production, marketing and sales in the newly emerged markets outside North America.

Such an option is especially available to those companies, investing in research and development to create a quality advantage in the market allowing for premium pricing.

**Continual improvement comes from combining passion with the ethics of workplace safety, urban living and a healthy environment.**

Continual improvement stimulated a Japanese corporation to give the market electronic products such as transistor radios, televisions, audio cassette players, video cassette players and ultimately creating the revolutionary portable cassette player with headphones.

The current revolution appears to be in the field of social media websites, shifting society from geographical markets to cyber markets. Once again, passion is helping us break out of the mold, creating new markets.

The very definition of market is challenged. It is no longer a trading place, but rather a medium through which business is transacted. Stock market floors have become silent as brokers sit behind computer screens punching out buy and sell orders.

Very often, the markets tend to identify a business with its latest successful product, when in fact this product represents the crowning glory in a series of successes.

**Noticing changes before your competition and adapting to the new circumstances is critical in continual business success.**

A major feature that has allowed long established corporations to continue to reinvent themselves is the ability to abandon feudalism and move towards a democratic management system that values professionalism.

Wisdom of embracing change and a determination to go global, have led to successful businesses being able to see opportunities where others see chaos.

Since the 1980s, the middleclass around the world has come of age inspired by success stories of information technology and global manufacturing.

**A strong and vocal middleclass values honesty.**

We have from our experience noted a confluence of business practices between multinational corporations from established economies operating in Asia and Africa, and local businesses.

An interesting story comes to mind of a major oil corporation using a large banner across gas stations on the highway in an Asian country advertising clean washrooms.

This was done to successfully entice travelers to drive in to top up on gas while utilizing the clean washrooms. Not surprisingly, this practice was picked up by other local businesses including restaurants.

We have noted that one of the ways to identify if staff are being treated well is to first check the conditions of the staff restroom at the work place. People who feel uneasy at the work place tend to be less productive.

MNCs including international franchise food chains have done a great service in many countries by introducing modern amenities for staff and customers thereby setting standards to be emulated. Global middleclass customers are very often attracted by the ambience of the premises in addition to the product and service.

This confluence of MNCs and local business practices has resulted in the creation of a pool of skilled individuals who have come to constitute the local middleclass. This middleclass has developed into a significant market and has in turn created numerous local businesses adopting business practices of multinational corporations.

A post 2008 trend has been, for local businesses in these emerged markets, to adopt a global productivity mindset to access markets worldwide.

With the right mindset, businesses will be able to protect market share in local markets and expand into new markets worldwide.

To do this, very often the talk turns to cost reduction. The tendency is, to start off with an existing established model and remove the redundant ingredients or components.

A few years back, a renowned international airline saved millions of dollars per year by simply removing one olive from every meal. In this context, the quality of the meal was compromised to a minimal effect.

However, there are instances, when cost cutting leads to compromising the quality to such an extent that even safety is overlooked.

The time tested principles, such as lean manufacturing and cleaner production have helped businesses to identify unnecessary or unwanted processes and eliminate them to reduce waste and thus reduce cost. But there is always a danger in starting from an existing model and working backwards.

Interestingly, the inventors of the light bulb, the personal computer and the world's cheapest car, all had the mindset of applying simplicity or lean engineering to create new products and experiences through innovation.

Training programs can help internalize a changed mindset. This can lead either to a closed loop profit circle or an upward improvement spiral through innovation.

**Internalize mindset change by leading the team through the process diagram.**

Give the team an *insight* into the importance of change. This allows the team to appreciate the *wisdom* of change which then acts as an *inspiration* that stimulates *interest*. Once the team members become *interested*, impart the *information* to allow individual team members to take *ownership* of processes.

This can lead to improved *performance*, increased *productivity* and *competitiveness* on a continual upward spiral.

## Process Diagram

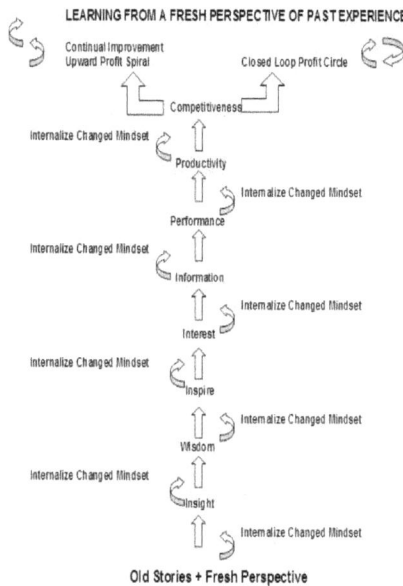

LEARNING FROM A FRESH PERSPECTIVE OF PAST EXPERIENCE

Continual Improvement Upward Profit Spiral

Closed Loop Profit Circle

Competitiveness

Internalize Changed Mindset

Productivity

Internalize Changed Mindset

Performance

Internalize Changed Mindset

Information

Internalize Changed Mindset

Interest

Internalize Changed Mindset

Inspire

Internalize Changed Mindset

Wisdom

Internalize Changed Mindset

Insight

Internalize Changed Mindset

Old Stories + Fresh Perspective

## Actionable Takeaway:

**Adopt a 'Continual Improvement Mindset' to avoid getting trapped into a closed loop cycle and, instead shift your team towards a continual improvement profit spiral upwards.**

## GLOBAL MIDDLECLASS MINDSET

*We need to understand that emerged markets exist within rapidly emerging economies and we now have a global middleclass that demands global quality standards.*

## CHAPTER 10 – Global Middleclass Mindset

The post 2008 global economic framework saw the emergence of G20 nations coordinating and stabilizing financial markets. Post 2020 with the emergence of the middleclass in various regions globally, we see a focus on building supply chain resilience.

**Businesses with a global productivity mindset succeed by delivering the quality demanded by the global middleclass.**

This middleclass began to emerge very rapidly within the 'tiger' economies of Asia from the 1980s onwards.

They were joined by the rapidly emerging middleclass in India, China, Brazil, South Africa and Russia.

The 1997 Asian financial crisis tested the resilience of this middleclass and the institutions, both government and private sector. This suggests that the middleclass of the G20 nations now constitute an emerged global middleclass who are demanding world class quality in products and services.

We now see MNCs from G7 countries finding huge profits by tapping into opportunities in the G20 markets. Even as business slows down in their home country, these MNCs have been able to increase sales in Asia, Africa and South America.

Over a decade ago, we saw a major coffee chain announce closing of outlets in the home country while planning to open more than twice as many new outlets in newly emerged markets. A global productivity mindset is what enables MNCs to respond at a global level, where a downturn in one market may happen simultaneously while there is an uptrend in another market, affording them opportunity.

During the lockdown owing to Covid-19 pandemic, those local restaurants that practiced global productivity mindset, were able to very rapidly shut down servicing customers in the restaurants, pivoting to home delivery.

It is quite certain that in the post 2008 world, the G20 markets are driving the global economy. The foundation of this economy is the middleclass demanding world class products and services. This trajectory of growth is anticipated to continue post 2023, notwithstanding the lockdown due to the global pandemic.

Productivity standards have now become the essence of profitability.

There appears to be a 70% - 30% rule operating where, in the established economies about 70% of the population may be part of the global middleclass consumers, but in the emerging and emerged economies only about 30% may be part of the global middleclass consumers.

However, this 30% in the emerging and emerged economies are significant in their numbers providing a huge market. Additionally, they act as drivers that shape the aspirations of the remaining 70% of the population striving to join the middleclass.

The policy makers and politicians in North America, including Canada, clearly recognize these realities. They are encouraging businesses big and small to seize these market opportunities even more vigorously.

President Obama in his address to the US Congress invoked America's drive to put a man on the moon as an example to encourage the spirit of innovation and enterprise.

The local middleclass may not possess the same spending power as the global middleclass, however, they represent a significant consumer group.

In huge population countries like India and China, a small margin of profit may add up to a large profit due to volume sales. Hence, the segmentation into mass and luxury markets.

With the advent of the internet and cyber connectivity, MNCs are becoming Trans National Corporations (TNCs) with the individual departments located in different parts of the world.

These TNCs are outsourcing as well as hiring the best human brains in the world thereby becoming multicultural corporations.

These two phenomena have turned the traditional brain drain into a brain network across geographical boundaries.

The idea of hiring the best requires a global sourcing for human talents that transforms successful organizations into multicultural communities. This requires skills in managing within the context of cultural diversity.

**Many business successes have been a result of actions based on utilizing global productivity mindset. This is the case with Grandma's satisfying meals, where she used this mindset without being aware of it.**

**In short, global productivity mindset is part of human nature and should become the foundation for productivity.**

It is not surprising that two of the most profitable business sectors worldwide are the financial and healthcare sectors.

In a crisis situation of 2008, the financial sector was able to contribute towards economic recovery by embracing a global productivity mindset. Similarly, in the crisis situation of 2020 pandemic lockdown, the healthcare sector was able to contribute towards public health recovery by embracing a global productivity mindset.

Essentially, embracing a global productivity mindset focuses industries on implementing their vision and mission through productive delivery of services and products.

Global productivity mindset helps us understand how the new global middleclass reality came about. It helps us benefit from this new global reality.

Productivity used to be, 'number of units per time or man-hours per unit'. Now the defining parameter is 'cost per unit delivered to consumer'. **Cost in today's**

**world includes impact on all stakeholders including the social and natural environment.**

An important objective is to be competitive so that the products (whether goods or services) are delivered to the customer, in the shortest possible lead time.

Due to globalization of trade, the competition is increasing in every field and the organizations with established and sustainable methods of process cost control become most competitive.

Thus, new global business practices must take into consideration production at the least possible cost with optimum quality in a transparent ethical business environment.

The global middleclass having access to information is now dictating quality standards. Right and wrong is based on the standards commonly accepted by society in general and the consumer in particular.

The organizations that successfully negated the 2008 meltdown and the 2020 pandemic lockdown were the ones adopting global productivity mindset. They reduced wastes in the processes without compromising on quality or environmental safety. These are the same organizations which can now focus on delivering higher quality at a better productivity level.

Global productivity mindset seeks to shape corporate culture and organizational behavior through the setting of clear guidelines on right and wrong action for the directors, managers and staff in a company thereby improving work ethics and attitude.

These ethical standards inform the stakeholders as to what the business represents within the society. The challenge is, to prevent corporate wrongs from destroying companies.

**A point to ponder is the fact that corporate scandals over the last three hundred years have essentially been about failures of human conduct and hence ethics.**

**Thus, a critical component of management in a global economy should be internal regulation within the corporation utilizing all the ten ingredients of the global productivity mindset.** It can be an effective instrument for the promotion of consumer confidence.

Global productivity mindset should be the underlying factor in all internal and external transactions and relationships.

Returning to the inspiration from Grandma, and the old spice trade that continues from ancient times, a pinch of enthusiasm, a dash of ambition and a large helping of hard work remains an excellent recipe for business success.

When it comes to identifying team leaders, it is important to note that one of the dichotomies of a leader's personality is that while he can be shy and reticent in social situations, he should be warm, outgoing and able to motivate teams at work.

**To motivate a team, we need to shape the mindset towards aspirations, desire to achieve, and a determination matching the ambition.**

Throughout history, multinational corporations have confirmed that hiring the best talent worldwide, and motivating through a global productivity mindset with a shared global vision, always succeeds.

This is because, productivity values are inherently human values, which transcend borders and local cultures.

Business success is best achieved by identifying the existing strengths in the organization from an outside perspective that gives the big picture. Learning from a fresh perspective of past experiences gives an insight to start the process of changing mindsets.

This big picture can promote **trade through training** of staff who can then take ownership of business processes to contribute towards achieving business excellence.

The issues raised in this book should form the basis for discussion, training and consulting from the Boardroom to the Shop floor in order to create a mindset for productivity that leads to human and financial profit within the realities of a post 2008 and especially in post 2020 global economy.

**Actionable Takeaway:**

*A 'Global Middleclass Mindset' helps us understand that the best way to benefit from worldwide markets is to stay focused on your vision and mission, with delivery taking into account local cultural expressions.*

# Appendix A

# EVOLUTION OF GLOBAL TRADE

## Europe ventures into Global Trade

*The 15<sup>th</sup> and 16<sup>th</sup> Centuries*

Global trade in spices, incense, cotton and dyes have existed across Asia to the Mediterranean for thousands of years prior to the 15<sup>th</sup> century. When conflict between Europe and West Asia threatened supply of commodities from Asia to Europe, states such as Portugal and Spain sent out ships in the hope of reaching the Indian commodities markets by navigating around Africa.

An attempt by Christopher Columbus to find a western sea route to India across the Atlantic Ocean led to European colonization of the Americas. Trade in new commodities such as chilies, potatoes, corn, cocoa and tobacco came to be established.

## Global Trade Expansion

*The 16<sup>th</sup> to the 19<sup>th</sup> Centuries*

These successes encouraged Britain and the Netherlands to join in this new sea trade between Europe and Asia. The British East India Company

(EIC) was chartered in 1600 with headquarters in London, England and operations based in Calcutta, India.

The EIC was the leading enterprise that came to dominate trade with Asia. This eventually led to the global commodities market shifting from India to London, England transforming the City of London into a global financial centre.

In North America the fur trade led to the charter of another British company known as the Hudson Bay Company (HBC) with headquarters in London, England and operations based in Winnipeg, Canada.

The HBC helped to open up North America through trade and settlement all the way to the Pacific West Coast.

The evolution of global free trade that now included Europe, Africa, Asia and the Americas was increasingly disrupted and complicated with the advent of European colonial political interference in Asia and the Americas.

In North America this colonial interference led to a war in 1776 which resulted in the creation of the United States of America (US).

Similarly, in India this colonial interference resulted in a war in 1857 seen as the first War of Indian Independence. Subsequently, India too gained independence in 1947, through a non-violent war on human conscience led by Mahatma Gandhi.

Despite all these political turbulences, global trade continued to grow under a colonial political and financial framework.

## Evolution of International Trade

*1900 – 1989*

At the dawn of the 20th century labor rights in Britain and the US began to establish fair wages for workers transforming the working class masses into a growing middleclass of consumers.

Armed with purchasing power and political determination to secure housing, education and health benefits this middleclass began the transformation of Europe and North America into middleclass consumer societies.

The end of the First World War in 1918 accelerated the process.

The end of the Second World War in 1945 saw similar aspirations amongst the peoples of Africa and Asia that led to the rise of nationalism and the achievement of political independence.

The politics of socialism and conservatism created a framework of international institutions. These international institutions include the United Nations Organization (UN), the International Monetary Fund (IMF), the World Bank, and the General Agreement on Tariffs and Trade (GATT), that shaped a new system that allowed international trade to grow.

## Re-emergence of Global Trade

*1989 – 2008*

The end of the Cold War that divided the member countries of the North Atlantic Treaty Organization (NATO) from Warsaw Pact countries helped nations worldwide to focus increasingly on free trade as the basis for economic and political relations. Trade with traditional cultural partners such as the Commonwealth of Nations and the Francophone Nations expanded into trade with non-traditional partners.

Countries like Malaysia and Singapore that historically traded with Britain, the Commonwealth, the US and

Europe increased trade with newly emerging market economies such as China, Russia and Central Asia.

The US increasingly traded with China for manufactured goods and with India for information technology services.

The interconnection of the global financial system created connectivity between stock exchanges worldwide influencing business sentiments across borders.

The Asian economies have focused on creating a middleclass. The measure of progress is influenced by the Organization of Economic Cooperation and Development (OECD) indicators.

The financial markets of the Group of Seven (G7) nations in Europe, North America and Japan helped shape the financial instruments for a business driven Asian economic growth.

Productivity systems from Total Quality Management (TQM), International Organization for Standardization (ISO), Lean Manufacturing and Six Sigma have reinforced the need for an educated workforce equipped with skills training and motivated with the right productivity mindset.

# GLOBAL PRODUCTIVITY MINDSET INGREDIENTS

**Skills Resources Mindset**
*Use existing resources to seize new opportunities.*

**Global Picture Mindset**
*Remove compartments to focus on vision, mission and goals.*

**Constant Change Mindset**
*Benefit from change and innovation.*

**Global Economy Mindset**
*Local markets are a part of the global market.*

**Ethical Quality Mindset**
*Create trust in products and services.*

**Process Efficiency Mindset**
*Benefit from a global network of finance, production and marketing.*

**Productivity Motivation Mindset**
*Allow the best individuals in the team to shine.*

**Business Passion Mindset**
*Passion is a critical component in the production cycle.*

**Continual Improvement Mindset**
*Create a continual profit spiral upwards.*

**Global Middleclass Mindset**
*Tap into global demand for quality.*

# IDENTIFY TRAINING
# AND CONSULTING NEEDS

Internalizing the mindset for continual improvement spiral upward will benefit from the following initiatives by all individuals in the organization.

1.    Claiming Ownership of Processes


2.    Adopting An Ethical Attitude


3.    Being Passionate, Motivated and Innovative


You need an analysis and evaluation across the organization in order to identify and customize training and consulting needs.

# MINDSET EXERCISE

Have you changed the mindset across your business?

Has the change made your business more competitive?

Has the change consolidated existing and new markets?

**Embrace the Global Productivity Mindset
and thrive in the 21$^{st}$ century.**

# GLOSSARY OF
# FRAMEWORK ORGANIZATIONS

**United Nations Organization**
http://www.un.org/en/

**International Monetary Fund**
http://www.imf.org/external/index.htm

**The World Bank**
http://www.worldbank.org/

**World Trade Organization**
http://www.wto.org/

**Organization of Economic Cooperation and Development**
http://www.oecd.org/home/

**Group of 7 Nations/G8 Summit 2012**
state.gov/e/eb/ecosum/2012g8/index.htm

**Group of 20 Nations**
http://www.g20.org/index.php/en/g20

**Commonwealth of Nations**
http://www.thecommonwealth.org/

**Organisation de la Francophonie**
http://www.francophonie.org/English.html

# RESEARCH REFERENCES

**Softwood lumber exports to China shatter record**
Newsroom.gov.bc.ca : February 16, 2012

**Perween Warsi: True grit got my samosas into Asda**
Moneyweek.com : Nov 20, 2009

**Special report:**
The new middle classes in emerging markets
**Burgeoning bourgeoisie**
The Economist : Feb 12th 2009

**Japan rated tops for innovation**
The Japan Times: Thursday, May 17, 2007

**What Can Tata's Nano Teach Detroit?**
By Jessie Scanlon
Businessweek.com/innovate/content/mar2009

**Tata Consultancy Services crosses $10bn in revenues**
BBC NEWS - BUSINESS: 23 April 2012

**Start-up Stories: NR Narayana Murthy, Infosys**
BBC NEWS - BUSINESS: 4 April 2011

**Future of Chinese economy in hands of consumer culture**
BBC NEWS – BUSINESS: 8 December 2011

**Kentucky Fried China - U.S. chicken franchise sales boom in world's most populous country**
Associated Press - 1/17/2005

**KFC's Radical Approach to China**
Harvard Business Review – November 2011

**Obama's state of the union address: US must seize 'Sputnik moment'**
The Guardian, UK: January 26, 2011

**Worldwide Financial Crisis Largely Bypasses Canada**
The Washington Post - October 16, 2008

**Financial Crisis Was Avoidable, Inquiry Finds**
The New York Times - January 25, 2011

**JPMorgan's Big Loss: Why Banks Still Haven't Learned Their Lesson**
Published: May 23, 2012 in Knowledge@Wharton

**Report on Deadly Factory Collapse in Bangladesh Finds Widespread Blame**
The New York Times – May 23, 2013

**The Rana Plaza disaster ten years on: What has changed?**
InfoStories – ILO - Published in April 2023

# Global Productivity Mindset
## Inspire Talent And Achieve
## Exceptional Performance

## AUTHORS

**Siddha Param,** LL.B. (Hons) (London), CLP(M) is a strategy and negotiation consultant with over 33 years experience advising Multinational Corporations as well as Micro, Small & Medium sized Enterprises on leadership, international business negotiations, dispute resolution and high performance. His experiences with clients from Europe, Asia, Africa and North America gives him a deep understanding of how to work across cultures. He teaches "Negotiation Theory & Practice" at Canadian Mennonite University/University of Winnipeg.
siddha.param@strandridge.com

**Prashant Tipnis**, is certified Lean Greenbelt Champion, Canada; Change Management, USA and Environmental Auditor in Kenya. His over 30 years of multicultural experience includes Operations and General Management; Project Implementation and Management and other significant leadership roles in India, Middle East Asia, East Africa, and Canada He has presided over various technical committees and social service organizations and has delivered presentations to industries and management institutions worldwide. Based in Winnipeg, Canada, he is utilizing his vast multi-tasking cross cultural experience in consulting, coaching and training. He teaches Managing Operations at the University of Winnipeg and Leadership Development at the Red River College, Winnipeg.
technolean@gmail.com

The authors believe that the current global economy offers tremendous opportunities for businesses that have a fresh perspective of past experiences.

The authors are in the business of promoting:

### Consulting to Identify Improvements
~
### Training to Sustain Improvements

www.ingramcontent.com/pod-product-compliance
Lightning Source LLC
Chambersburg PA
CBHW071213200326
41519CB00018B/5507